LITTLE FLOW

Instructions on page 49.

1

2   Instructions on page 50.

Instructions on page 51.

4

Instructions on page 52.

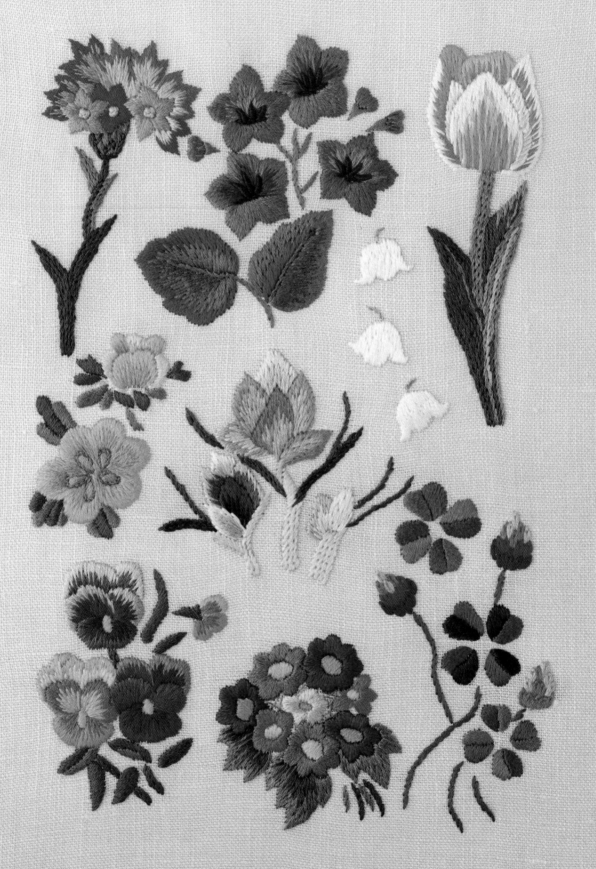

Instructions on page 53.

6　　　　　　　　　Instructions on page 54.

8   Instructions on page 56.

Instructions on page 57

Instructions on page 58.

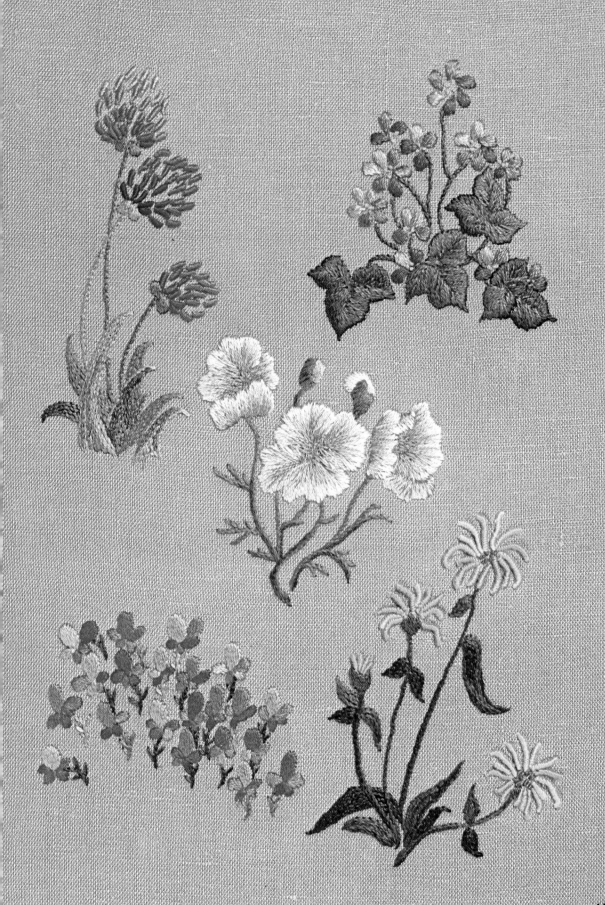

Instructions on page 59.

Instructions on page 60.

Instructions on page 62.

Instructions on page 63

16   Instructions on page 64.

Instructions on page 65

18   Instructions on page 66.

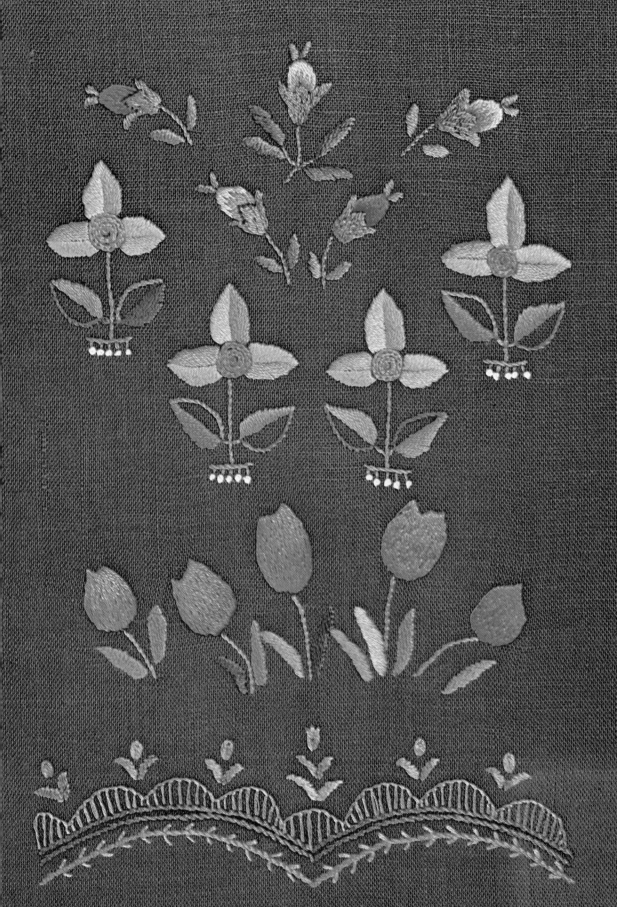

Instructions on page 67

Instructions on page 68

Instructions on page 70.

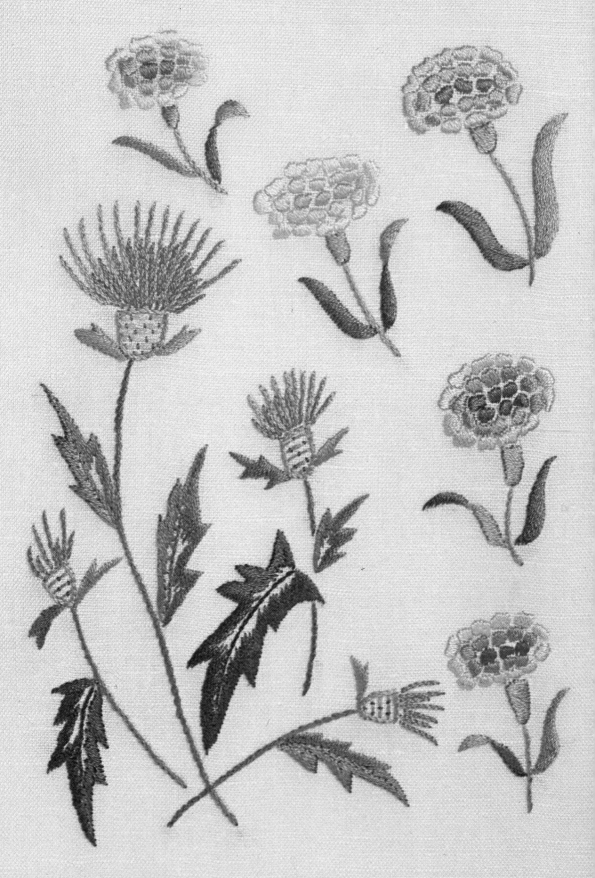

Instructions on page 72.

BIRDS AND ANIMALS

Instructions on page 74.

Instructions on page 75.

Instructions on page 76.

30

Instructions on page 78.

Instructions on page 79.

Instructions on page 80

ONE-POINT EMBROIDERY

Instructions on page 82.

Instructions on page 84.

Instructions on page 86.

Instructions on page 87.

Instructions on page 88

FLOWERS' CHAT

Instructions on page 89.

Instructions on page 90.

Instructions on page 91

44

Instructions on page 92

FLORAL INITIALS

Instructions on page 94.

JOLLY EMBLEMS

Instructions on page 95.

Instructions on page 96

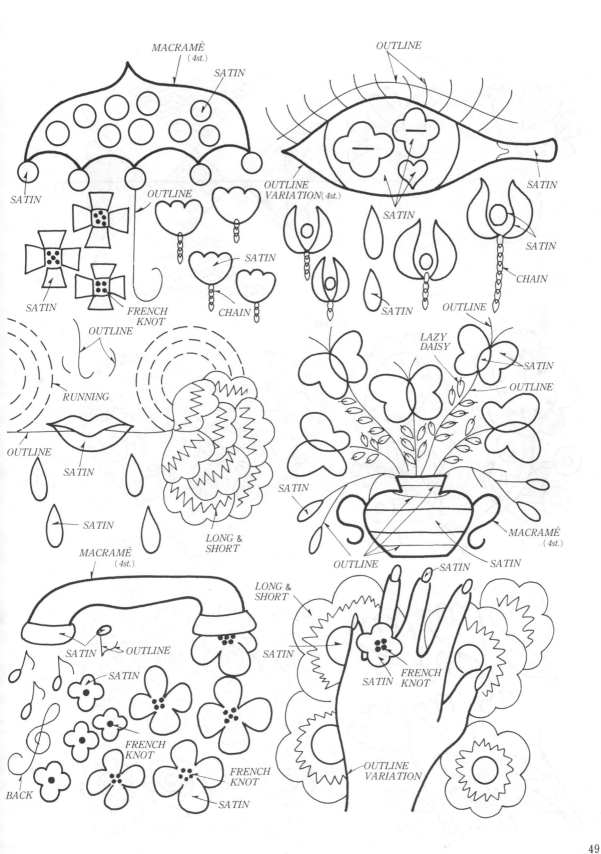

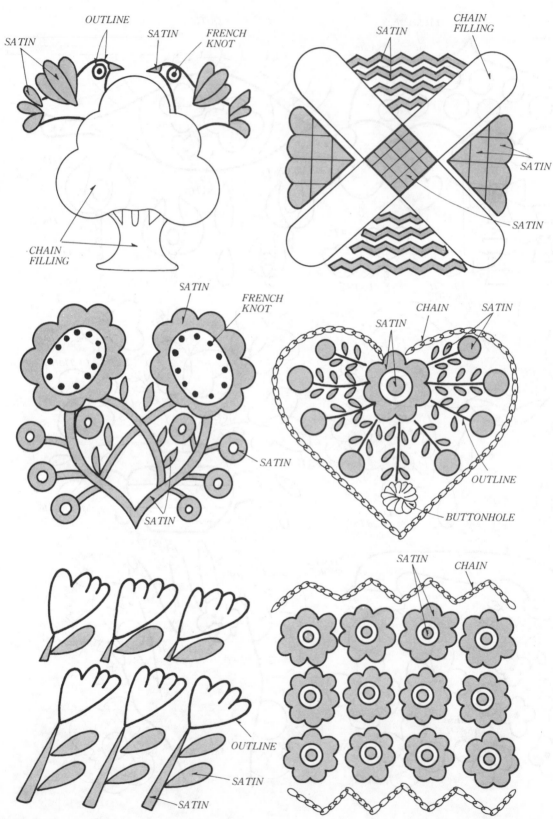

NEEDLEWORK on page 3.   *3 strands, unless otherwise specified.*

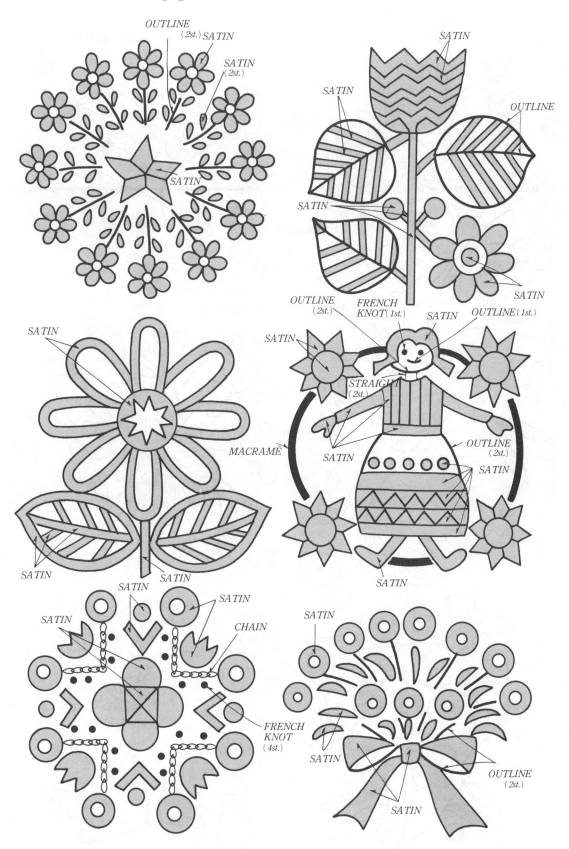

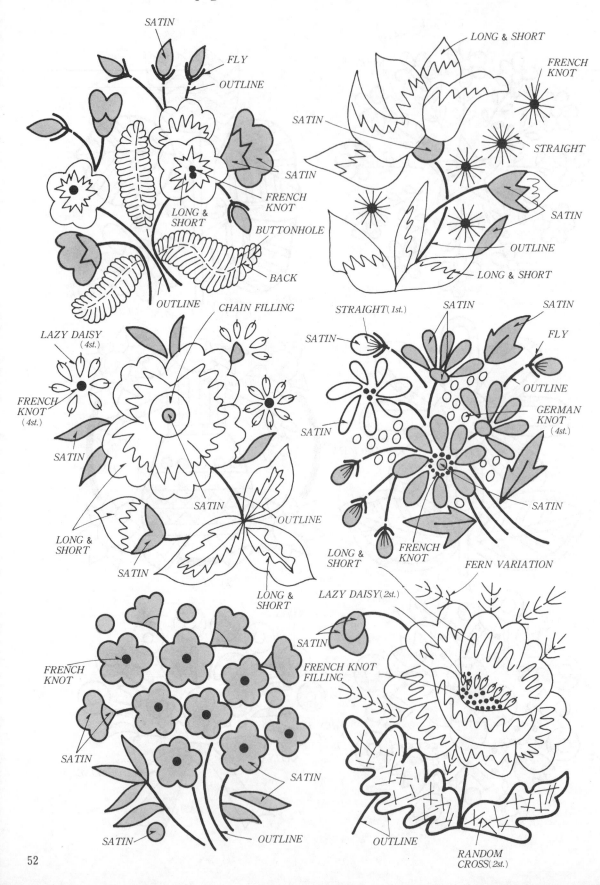

3 strands, unless otherwise specified.

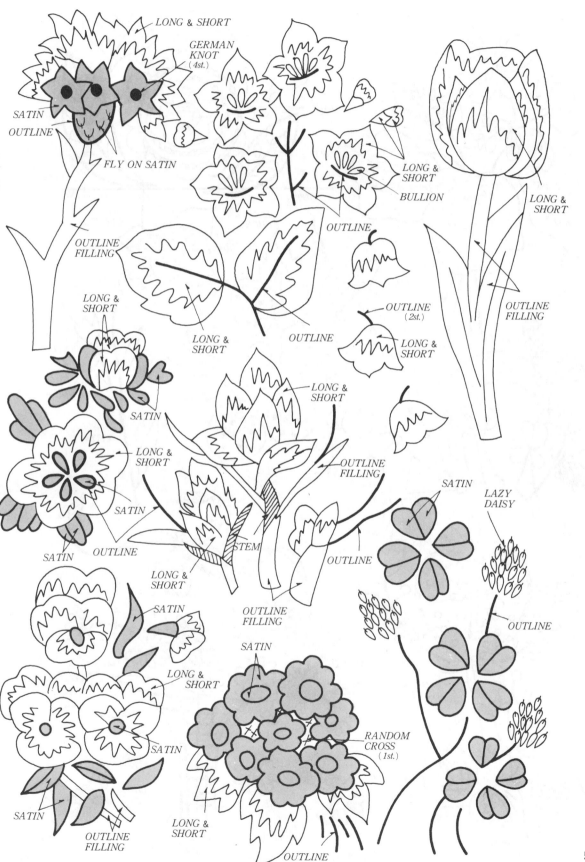

LONG & SHORT

GERMAN KNOT (4st.)

SATIN

OUTLINE

FLY ON SATIN

LONG & SHORT

BULLION

LONG & SHORT

OUTLINE FILLING

LONG & SHORT

OUTLINE

LONG & SHORT

OUTLINE FILLING

OUTLINE

LONG & SHORT

LONG & SHORT

SATIN

OUTLINE (2st.)

LONG & SHORT

LONG & SHORT

SATIN

OUTLINE FILLING

SATIN

LAZY DAISY

LONG & SHORT

SATIN

SATIN

OUTLINE

STEM

OUTLINE

SATIN

LONG & SHORT

SATIN

OUTLINE FILLING

SATIN

LONG & SHORT

RANDOM CROSS (1st.)

OUTLINE

SATIN

OUTLINE FILLING

LONG & SHORT

OUTLINE

NEEDLEWORK on page 6.   *2 strands, unless otherwise specified.*

LAZY DAISY
(1st.)

BULLION

LONG &
SHORT

SATIN

SATIN

SATIN

LONG &
SHORT

OUTLINE

SATIN

CHAIN
(3st.)

SATIN

OUTLINE

SATIN

LAZY
DAISY (3st.)

SATIN

SATIN

OUTLINE

SATIN

OUTLINE

SATIN

OUTLINE
FILLING

OUTLINE

OUTLINE

LONG &
SHORT

OUTLINE

FRENCH
KNOT (3st.)

LONG & SHORT
(3st.)

SATIN

LONG &
SHORT

LONG &
SHORT

SATIN

BACK

SATIN

OUTLINE

SATIN

CHAIN
(3st.)

SATIN

CHAIN

OUTLINE

SATIN

CLOSED
HERRINGBONE

OUTLINE

OUTLINE FILLING
(4st.)

MACR-
AME (4st.)

PADDED
SATIN

SATIN
(3st.)

SATIN

GERMAN
KNOT
(4st.)

SATIN

OUTLINE (1st.)

SATIN
(3st.)

OUTLINE

SATIN

OUTLINE

MACRAMÉ
(4st.)

SATIN

OUTLINE
(3st.)

OUTLINE

PADDED
SATIN

LONG &
SHORT (3st.)

MACRAMÉ
(4st.)

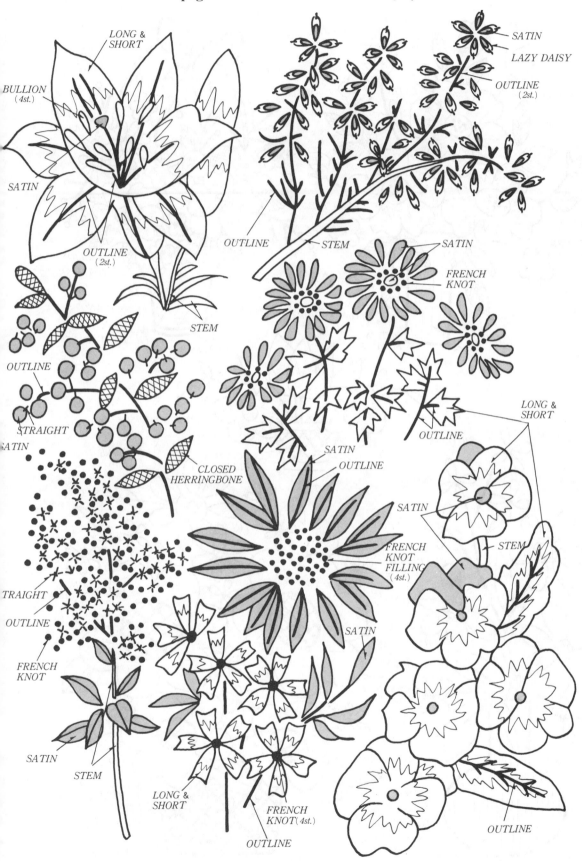

NEEDLEWORK on page 7.

3 strands, unless otherwise specified.

LONG & SHORT

SATIN

LAZY DAISY

BULLION (4st.)

OUTLINE (2st.)

SATIN

OUTLINE (2st.)

STEM

OUTLINE — STEM

SATIN

FRENCH KNOT

OUTLINE

STEM

OUTLINE

STRAIGHT

SATIN

CLOSED HERRINGBONE

OUTLINE

LONG & SHORT

SATIN

OUTLINE

SATIN

STEM

FRENCH KNOT FILLING (4st.)

SATIN

STRAIGHT

OUTLINE

FRENCH KNOT

SATIN

STEM

LONG & SHORT

FRENCH KNOT (4st.)

OUTLINE

OUTLINE

3 strands, unless otherwise specified.

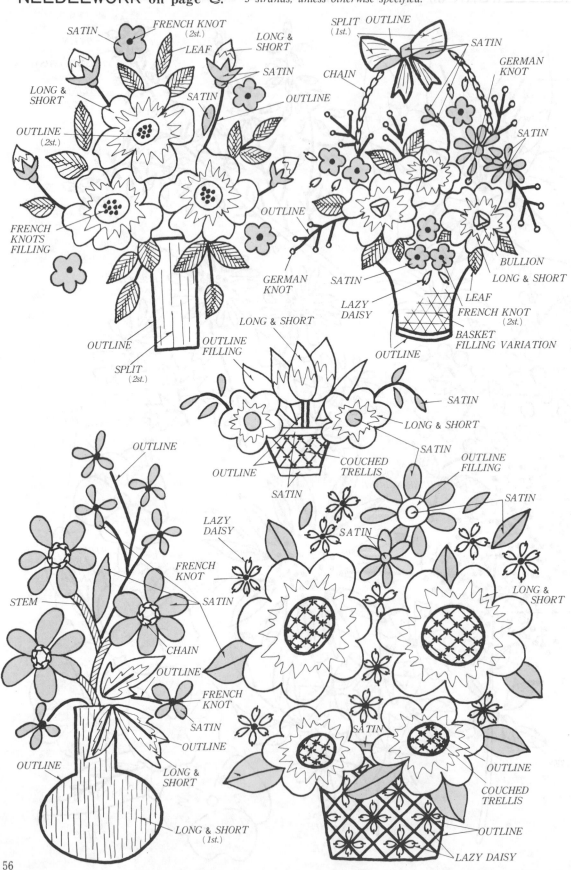

SATIN

FRENCH KNOT (2st.)

LEAF

LONG & SHORT

SATIN

LONG & SHORT

OUTLINE (2st.)

SATIN

SATIN

OUTLINE

FRENCH KNOTS FILLING

OUTLINE

OUTLINE

OUTLINE FILLING

SPLIT (2st.)

GERMAN KNOT

LONG & SHORT

SPLIT (1st.)

OUTLINE

CHAIN

SATIN

GERMAN KNOT

SATIN

BULLION

LONG & SHORT

SATIN

LEAF

FRENCH KNOT (2st.)

LAZY DAISY

OUTLINE

BASKET FILLING VARIATION

SATIN

LONG & SHORT

OUTLINE

SATIN

COUCHED TRELLIS

SATIN

OUTLINE FILLING

SATIN

LAZY DAISY

FRENCH KNOT

SATIN

SATIN

LONG & SHORT

OUTLINE

STEM

CHAIN

OUTLINE

FRENCH KNOT

SATIN

OUTLINE

LONG & SHORT

OUTLINE

LONG & SHORT (1st.)

SATIN

OUTLINE

COUCHED TRELLIS

OUTLINE

LAZY DAISY

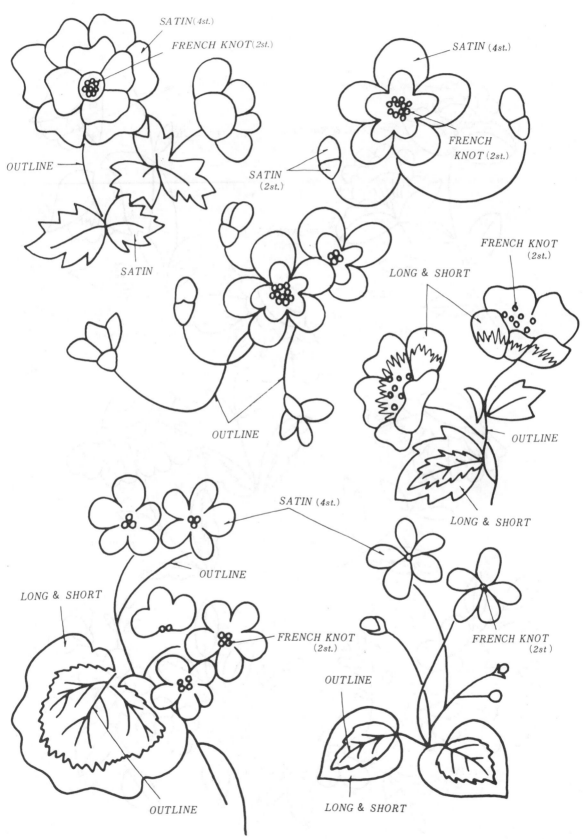

SATIN(4st.)

FRENCH KNOT(2st.)

SATIN (4st.)

OUTLINE

FRENCH KNOT (2st.)

SATIN (2st.)

SATIN

FRENCH KNOT (2st.)

LONG & SHORT

OUTLINE

OUTLINE

LONG & SHORT

SATIN (4st.)

OUTLINE

LONG & SHORT

FRENCH KNOT (2st.)

FRENCH KNOT (2st.)

OUTLINE

OUTLINE

LONG & SHORT

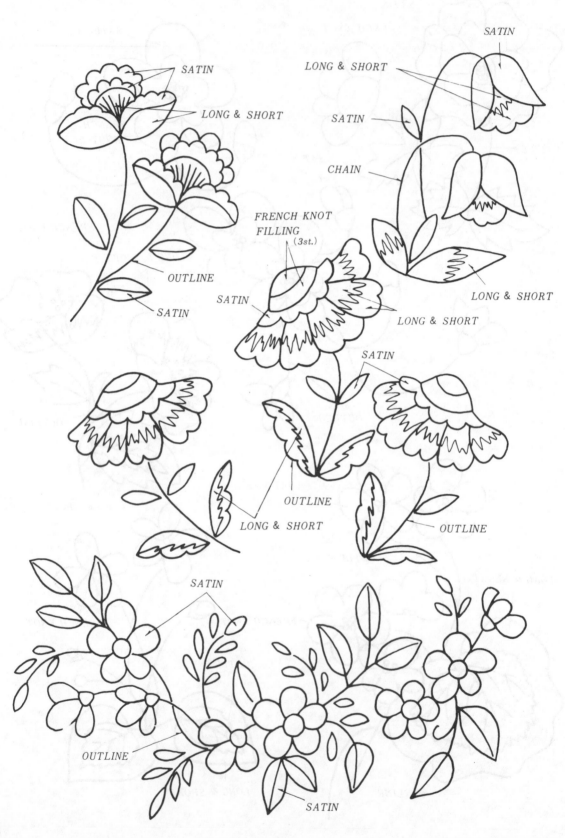

SATIN

LONG & SHORT

LONG & SHORT

SATIN

CHAIN

SATIN

SATIN

OUTLINE

SATIN

FRENCH KNOT
FILLING
(3st.)

SATIN

LONG & SHORT

LONG & SHORT

SATIN

OUTLINE

OUTLINE

LONG & SHORT

OUTLINE

SATIN

OUTLINE

SATIN

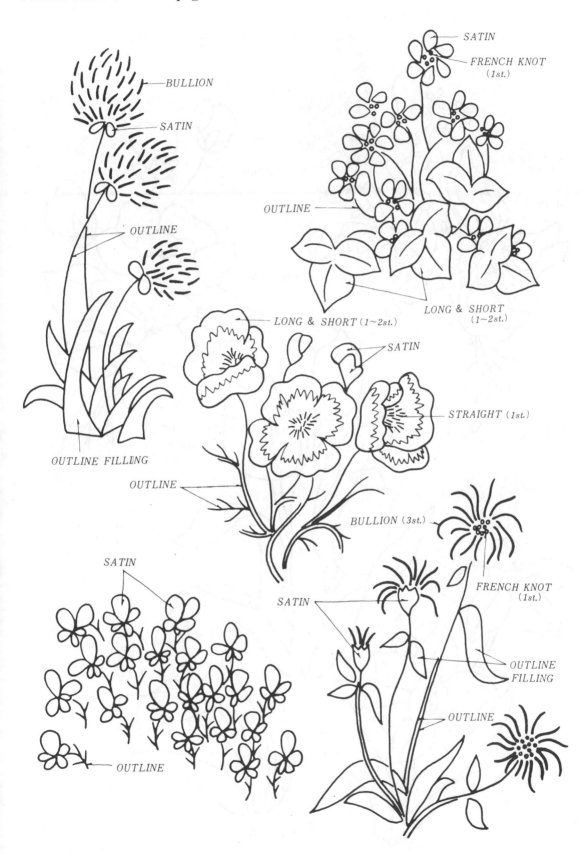

BULLION

SATIN

OUTLINE

OUTLINE FILLING

SATIN

FRENCH KNOT
(1st.)

OUTLINE

LONG & SHORT (1~2st.)

LONG & SHORT
(1~2st.)

SATIN

STRAIGHT (1st.)

OUTLINE

BULLION (3st.)

FRENCH KNOT
(1st.)

SATIN

SATIN

OUTLINE
FILLING

OUTLINE

OUTLINE

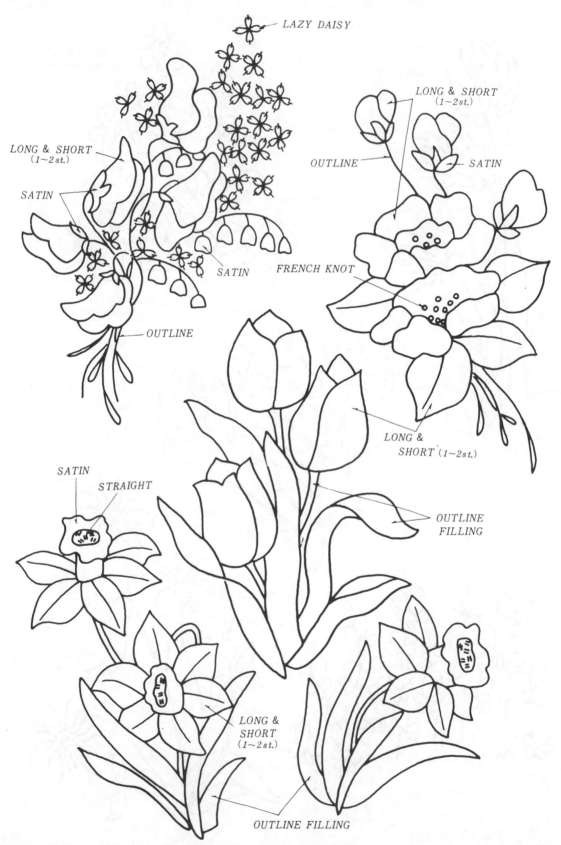

LAZY DAISY

LONG & SHORT
(1~2st.)

LONG & SHORT
(1~2st.)

OUTLINE

SATIN

SATIN

SATIN

FRENCH KNOT

OUTLINE

LONG &
SHORT (1~2st.)

SATIN

STRAIGHT

OUTLINE
FILLING

LONG &
SHORT
(1~2st.)

OUTLINE FILLING

NEEDLEWORK **on page 13.** *3 strands, unless otherwise specified.*

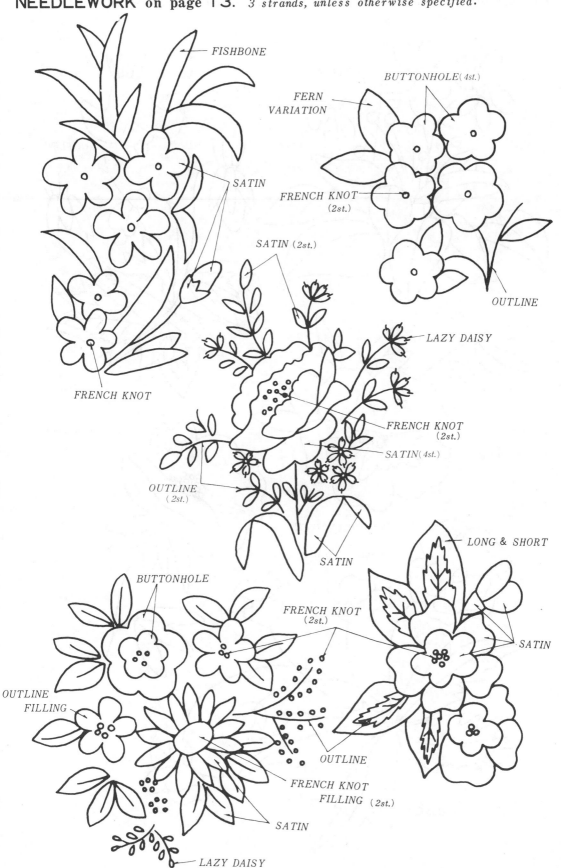

FISHBONE

BUTTONHOLE(4st.)

FERN
VARIATION

SATIN

FRENCH KNOT
(2st.)

SATIN (2st.)

OUTLINE

LAZY DAISY

FRENCH KNOT
(2st.)

SATIN(4st.)

FRENCH KNOT

OUTLINE
(2st.)

SATIN

LONG & SHORT

BUTTONHOLE

FRENCH KNOT
(2st.)

SATIN

OUTLINE
FILLING

OUTLINE

FRENCH KNOT
FILLING (2st.)

SATIN

LAZY DAISY

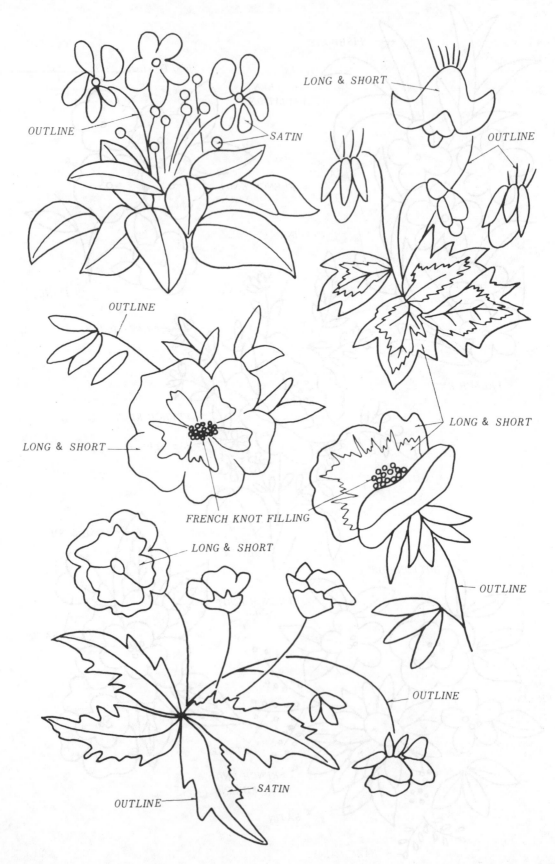

OUTLINE

SATIN

LONG & SHORT

OUTLINE

OUTLINE

LONG & SHORT

OUTLINE

LONG & SHORT

LONG & SHORT

FRENCH KNOT FILLING

LONG & SHORT

OUTLINE

OUTLINE

SATIN

OUTLINE

NEEDLEWORK on page 15. *3 strands, unless otherwise specified.*

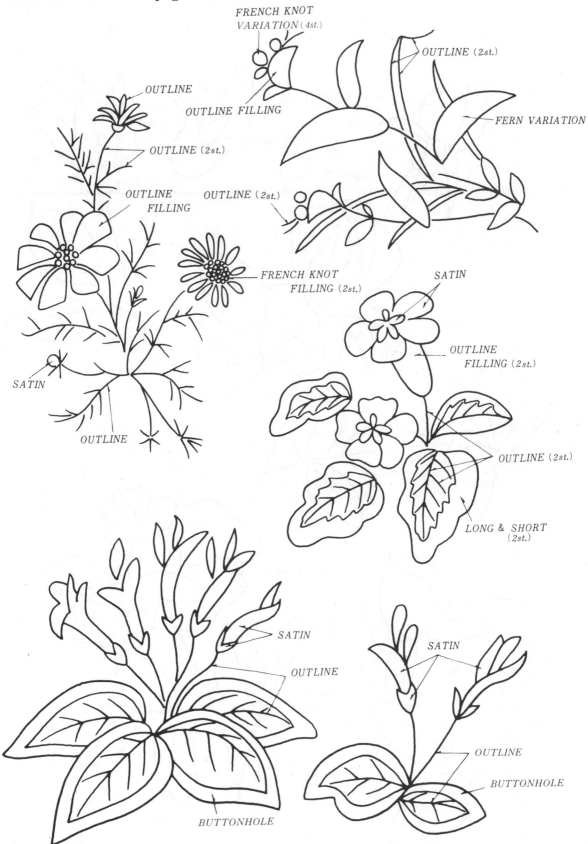

FRENCH KNOT
VARIATION (4st.)

OUTLINE

OUTLINE FILLING

OUTLINE (2st.)

FERN VARIATION

OUTLINE (2st.)

OUTLINE
FILLING

OUTLINE (2st.)

OUTLINE (2st.)

FRENCH KNOT
FILLING (2st.)

SATIN

OUTLINE
FILLING (2st.)

SATIN

OUTLINE

OUTLINE (2st.)

LONG & SHORT
(2st.)

SATIN

OUTLINE

SATIN

OUTLINE

BUTTONHOLE

BUTTONHOLE

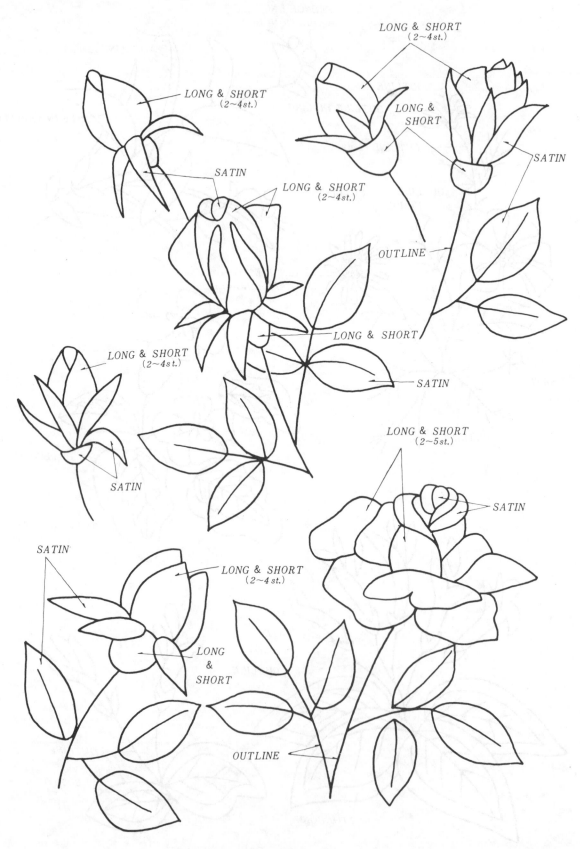

LONG & SHORT
(2~4 st.)

LONG & SHORT
(2~4st.)

LONG & SHORT

SATIN

SATIN

LONG & SHORT
(2~4st.)

SATIN

LONG & SHORT
(2~4st.)

OUTLINE

LONG & SHORT

LONG & SHORT
(2~4st.)

SATIN

SATIN

LONG & SHORT
(2~5st.)

SATIN

LONG & SHORT
(2~4 st.)

SATIN

LONG
&
SHORT

OUTLINE

2 strands, unless otherwise specified.

OUTLINE

STRAIGHT

OUTLINE
(3st.)

SATIN

FRENCH
KNOT
(3st.)

FRENCH KNOT
(3st.)

SATIN

SATIN

OUTLINE
(3st.)

LAZY DAISY
(3st.)

OUTLINE

SATIN

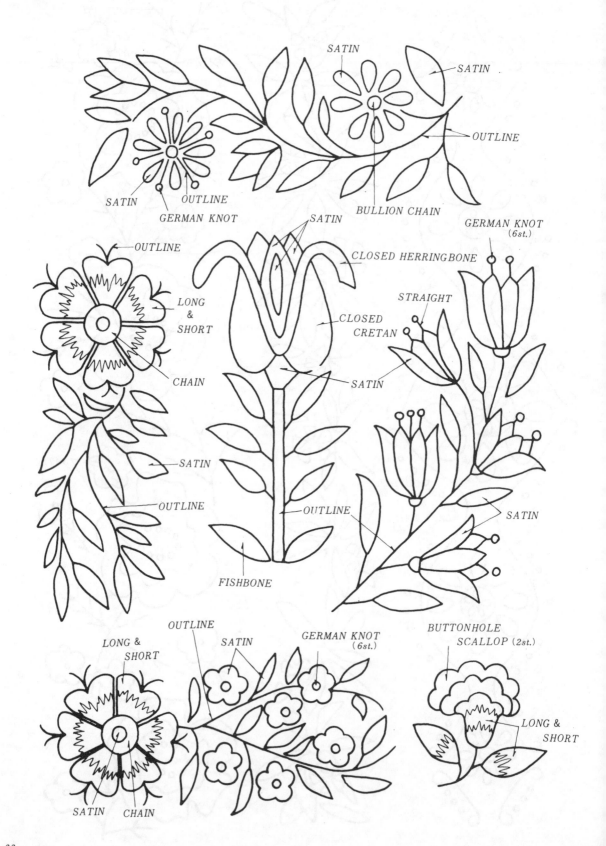

SATIN

SATIN

OUTLINE

SATIN   OUTLINE

GERMAN KNOT

BULLION CHAIN

GERMAN KNOT
(6st.)

SATIN

CLOSED HERRINGBONE

STRAIGHT

OUTLINE

LONG
&
SHORT

CLOSED
CRETAN

CHAIN

SATIN

SATIN

OUTLINE

SATIN

OUTLINE

FISHBONE

SATIN

OUTLINE

LONG &
SHORT

SATIN

GERMAN KNOT
(6st.)

BUTTONHOLE
SCALLOP (2st.)

LONG &
SHORT

SATIN   CHAIN

66

2 *strands, unless otherwise specified.*

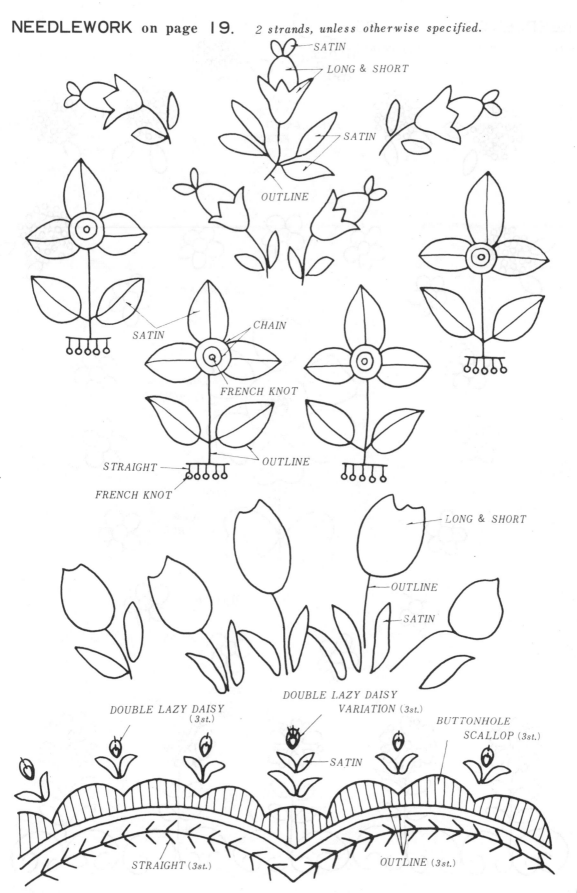

SATIN

LONG & SHORT

SATIN

OUTLINE

SATIN

CHAIN

FRENCH KNOT

STRAIGHT — OUTLINE

FRENCH KNOT

LONG & SHORT

OUTLINE

SATIN

DOUBLE LAZY DAISY
VARIATION (3st.)

DOUBLE LAZY DAISY
(3st.)

BUTTONHOLE
SCALLOP (3st.)

SATIN

STRAIGHT (3st.)

OUTLINE (3st.)

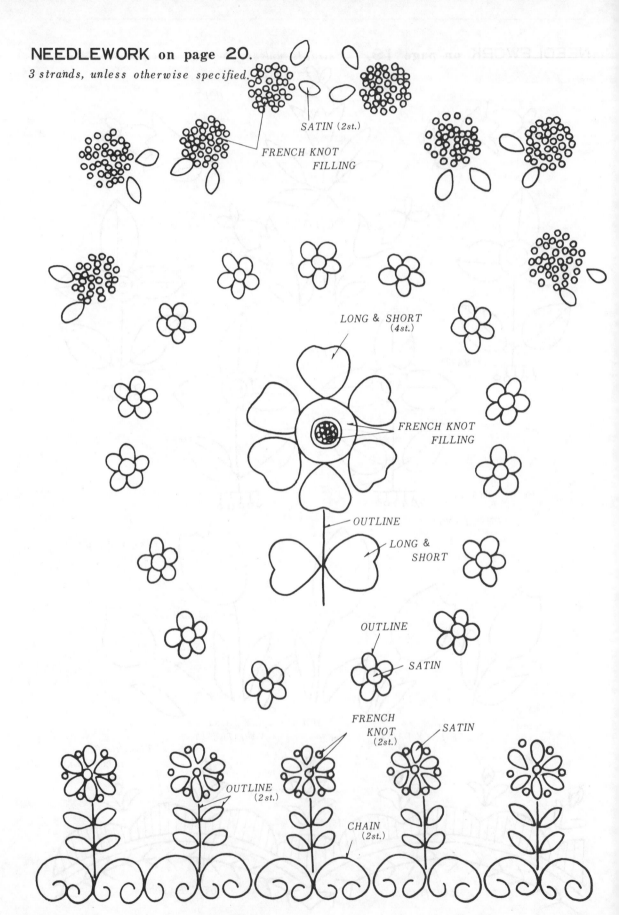

NEEDLEWORK on page 20.

3 strands, unless otherwise specified.

SATIN (2st.)

FRENCH KNOT
FILLING

LONG & SHORT
(4st.)

FRENCH KNOT
FILLING

OUTLINE

LONG &
SHORT

OUTLINE

SATIN

FRENCH
KNOT
(2st.)

SATIN

OUTLINE
(2st.)

CHAIN
(2st.)

NEEDLEWORK on page 21. *3 strands, unless otherwise specified.*

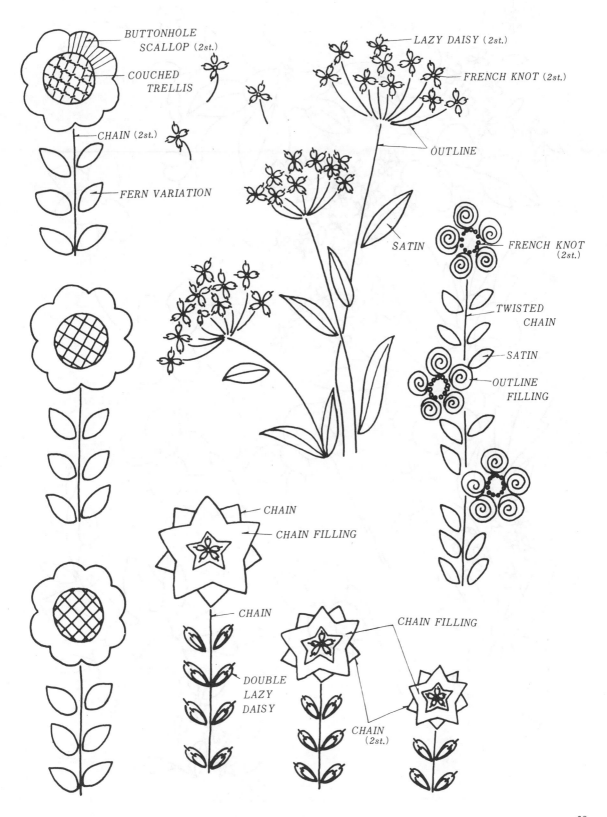

BUTTONHOLE SCALLOP (2st.)

COUCHED TRELLIS

CHAIN (2st.)

FERN VARIATION

LAZY DAISY (2st.)

FRENCH KNOT (2st.)

OUTLINE

SATIN

FRENCH KNOT (2st.)

TWISTED CHAIN

SATIN

OUTLINE FILLING

CHAIN

CHAIN FILLING

CHAIN

DOUBLE LAZY DAISY

CHAIN FILLING

CHAIN (2st.)

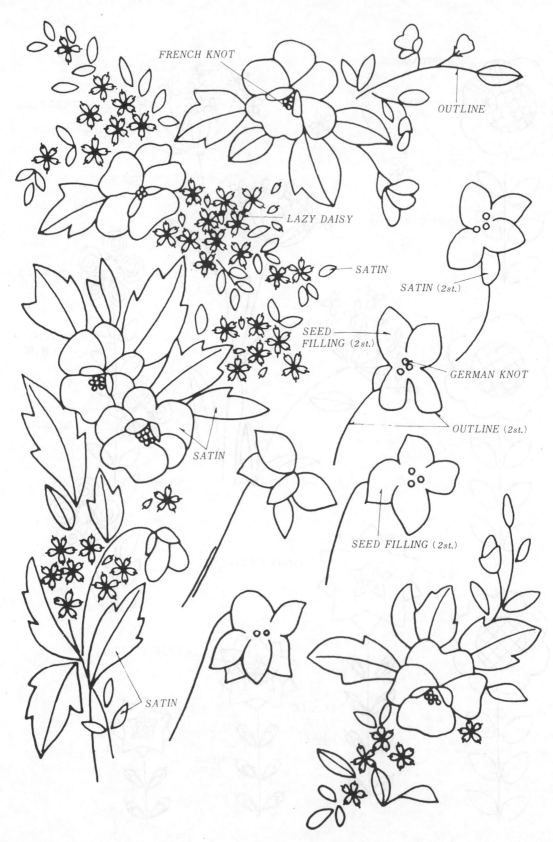

FRENCH KNOT

OUTLINE

LAZY DAISY

SATIN

SATIN (2st.)

SEED
FILLING (2st.)

GERMAN KNOT

OUTLINE (2st.)

SATIN

SEED FILLING (2st.)

SATIN

FRENCH KNOT

LAZY DAISY

OUTLINE

CHAIN

FERN VARIATION

SATIN (4st.)

BUTTONHOLE

LAZY DAISY

BUTTONHOLE (4st.)

FRENCH
KNOT
(2st.)

SURFACE DARNING
(4st.)

FRENCH KNOT VARIATION
(4st.)

DOUBLE
LAZY DAISY

BUTTONHOLE

OUTLINE (2st.)

FERN VARIATION
(4st.)

CLOSED HERRINGBONE
(2st.)

FRENCH KNOT
VARIATION

OUTLINE
(2st)

FRENCH KNOT

FRENCH KNOT
VARIATION

LAZY DAISY
(3st.)

CHAIN

FRENCH KNOT

BUTTONHOLE
(3st.)

OUTLINE
(2st.)

LONG & SHORT
(2st.)

BUTTONHOLE

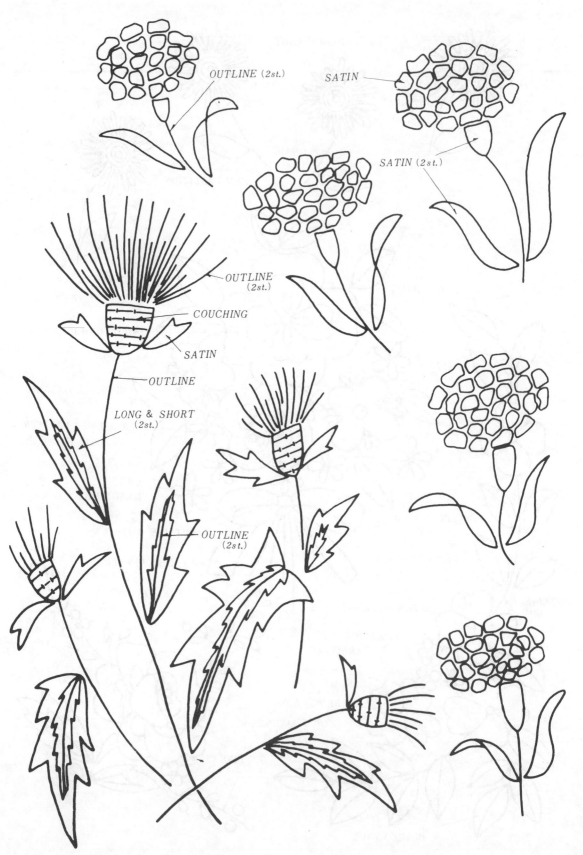

OUTLINE (2st.)

SATIN

SATIN (2st.)

OUTLINE
(2st.)

COUCHING

SATIN

OUTLINE

LONG & SHORT
(2st.)

OUTLINE
(2st.)

NEEDLEWORK on page 25. *2 strands, unless otherwise specified.*

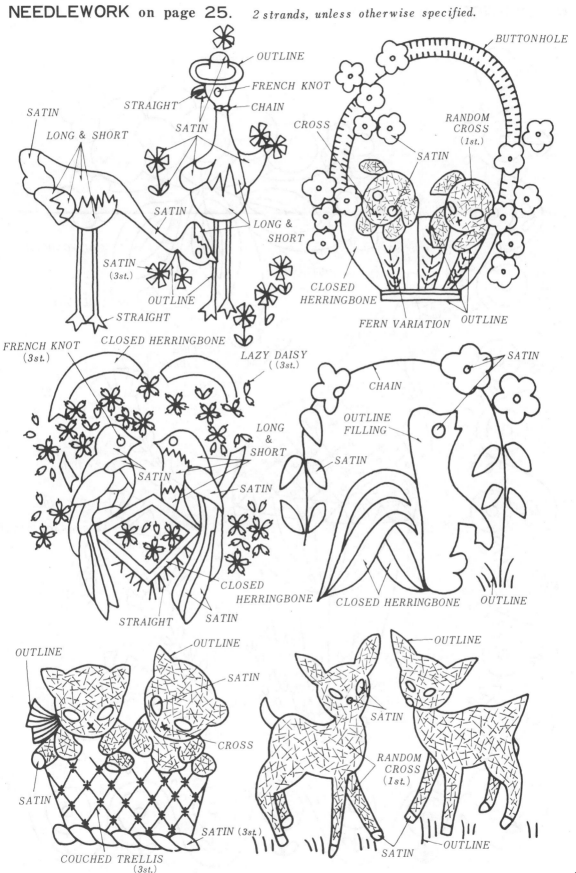

OUTLINE

FRENCH KNOT

STRAIGHT

CHAIN

SATIN

SATIN

LONG & SHORT

LONG & SHORT

SATIN

SATIN (3st.)

OUTLINE

STRAIGHT

BUTTONHOLE

CROSS

RANDOM CROSS (1st.)

SATIN

CLOSED HERRINGBONE

FERN VARIATION

OUTLINE

FRENCH KNOT (3st.)

CLOSED HERRINGBONE

LAZY DAISY ((3st.)

LONG & SHORT

SATIN

SATIN

SATIN

CLOSED HERRINGBONE

STRAIGHT

SATIN

CHAIN

SATIN

OUTLINE FILLING

SATIN

CLOSED HERRINGBONE

OUTLINE

OUTLINE

OUTLINE

SATIN

CROSS

SATIN

SATIN

COUCHED TRELLIS (3st.)

SATIN (3st)

OUTLINE

SATIN

RANDOM CROSS (1st.)

OUTLINE

SATIN

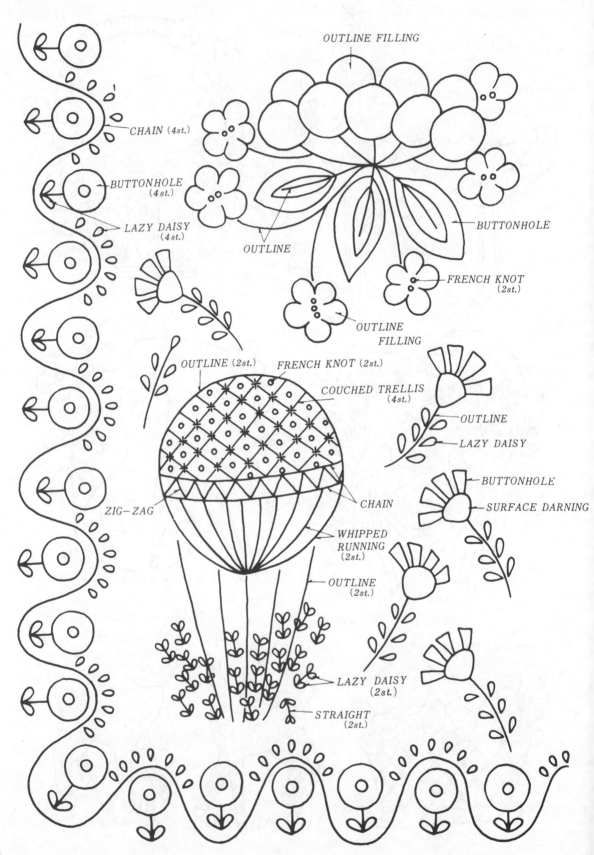

OUTLINE FILLING

CHAIN (4st.)

BUTTONHOLE (4st.)

LAZY DAISY (4st.)

OUTLINE

BUTTONHOLE

FRENCH KNOT (2st.)

OUTLINE FILLING

OUTLINE (2st.)

FRENCH KNOT (2st.)

COUCHED TRELLIS (4st.)

OUTLINE

LAZY DAISY

BUTTONHOLE

SURFACE DARNING

ZIG–ZAG

CHAIN

WHIPPED RUNNING (2st.)

OUTLINE (2st.)

LAZY DAISY (2st.)

STRAIGHT (2st.)

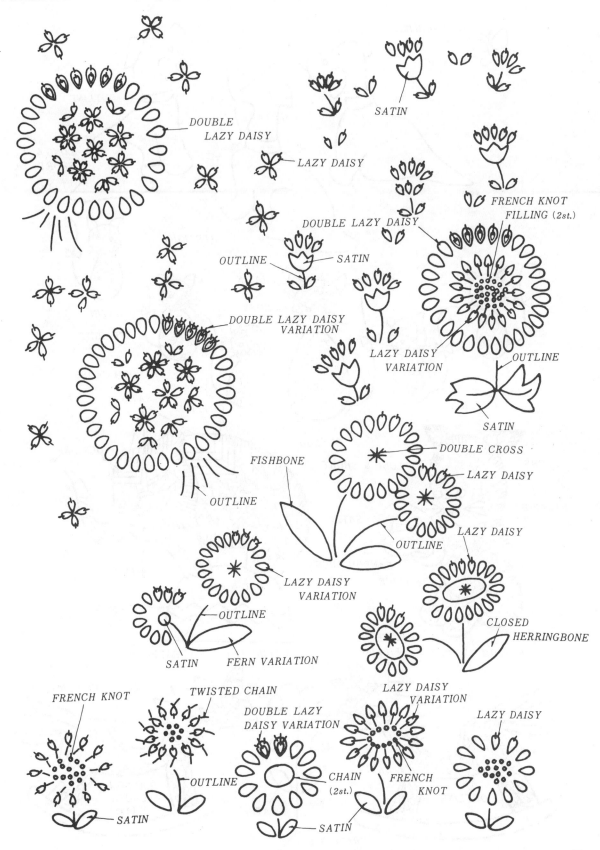

DOUBLE LAZY DAISY

SATIN

LAZY DAISY

FRENCH KNOT FILLING (2st.)

DOUBLE LAZY DAISY

OUTLINE

SATIN

DOUBLE LAZY DAISY VARIATION

LAZY DAISY VARIATION

OUTLINE

SATIN

DOUBLE CROSS

LAZY DAISY

FISHBONE

OUTLINE

OUTLINE

LAZY DAISY

LAZY DAISY VARIATION

LAZY DAISY

CLOSED HERRINGBONE

SATIN

OUTLINE

FERN VARIATION

FRENCH KNOT

TWISTED CHAIN

DOUBLE LAZY DAISY VARIATION

LAZY DAISY VARIATION

LAZY DAISY

OUTLINE

CHAIN (2st.)

FRENCH KNOT

SATIN

SATIN

NEEDLEWORK on page 28. *2 strands, unless otherwise specified.*

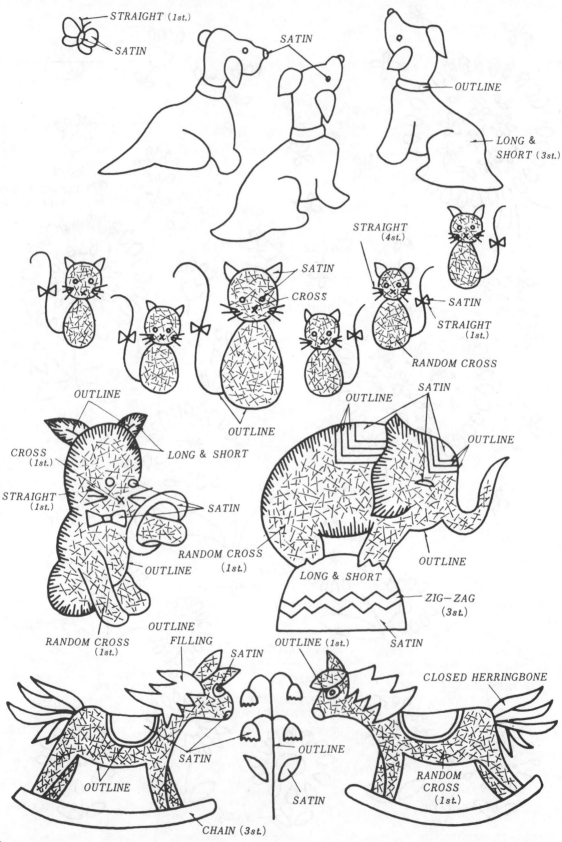

STRAIGHT (1st.)

SATIN

SATIN

OUTLINE

LONG & SHORT (3st.)

STRAIGHT (4st.)

SATIN

CROSS

SATIN

STRAIGHT (1st.)

RANDOM CROSS

OUTLINE

OUTLINE

SATIN

OUTLINE

OUTLINE

OUTLINE

CROSS (1st.)

LONG & SHORT

STRAIGHT (1st.)

SATIN

RANDOM CROSS (1st.)

OUTLINE

LONG & SHORT

OUTLINE

ZIG–ZAG (3st.)

RANDOM CROSS (1st.)

OUTLINE FILLING

OUTLINE (1st.)

SATIN

SATIN

SATIN

CLOSED HERRINGBONE

OUTLINE

OUTLINE

SATIN

RANDOM CROSS (1st.)

CHAIN (3st.)

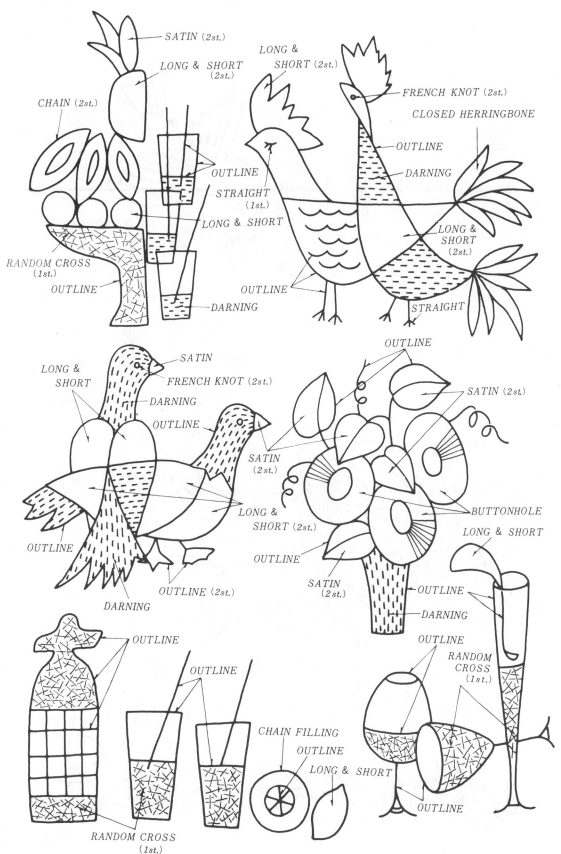

SATIN (2st.)

LONG & SHORT (2st.)

LONG & SHORT (2st.)

CHAIN (2st.)

FRENCH KNOT (2st.)

CLOSED HERRINGBONE

OUTLINE

DARNING

OUTLINE

STRAIGHT (1st.)

LONG & SHORT

LONG & SHORT (2st.)

RANDOM CROSS (1st.)

OUTLINE

OUTLINE

OUTLINE

STRAIGHT

DARNING

LONG & SHORT

SATIN

FRENCH KNOT (2st.)

DARNING

OUTLINE

OUTLINE

SATIN (2st.)

SATIN (2st.)

LONG & SHORT (2st.)

OUTLINE

BUTTONHOLE

LONG & SHORT

OUTLINE

OUTLINE (2st.)

DARNING

SATIN (2st.)

OUTLINE

DARNING

OUTLINE

OUTLINE

RANDOM CROSS (1st.)

OUTLINE

OUTLINE

CHAIN FILLING

OUTLINE

LONG & SHORT

RANDOM CROSS (1st.)

OUTLINE

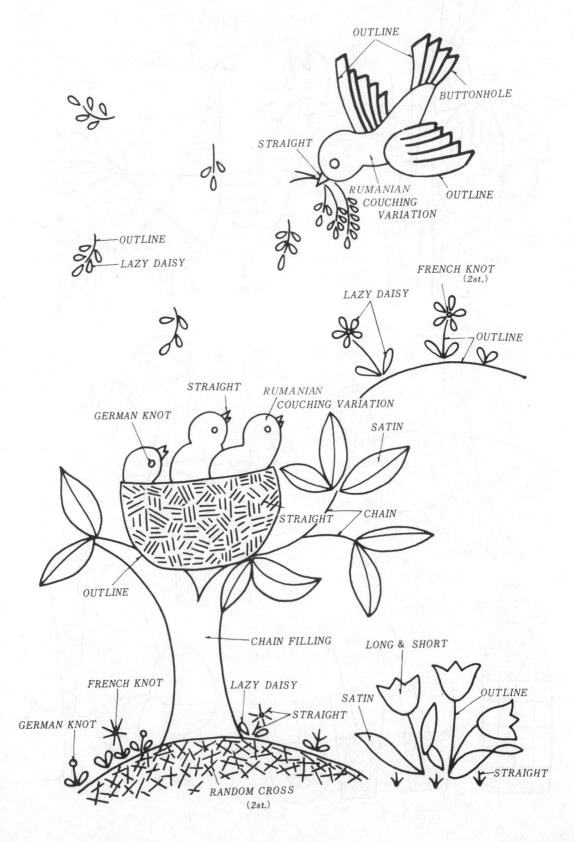

OUTLINE

BUTTONHOLE

STRAIGHT

RUMANIAN
COUCHING
VARIATION

OUTLINE

OUTLINE

LAZY DAISY

FRENCH KNOT
(2st.)

LAZY DAISY

OUTLINE

STRAIGHT

RUMANIAN
COUCHING VARIATION

SATIN

GERMAN KNOT

STRAIGHT

CHAIN

OUTLINE

CHAIN FILLING

LONG & SHORT

FRENCH KNOT

LAZY DAISY

SATIN

OUTLINE

GERMAN KNOT

STRAIGHT

STRAIGHT

RANDOM CROSS
(2st.)

SATIN

OUTLINE

STRAIGHT

OUTLINE

STRAIGHT (1st.)

STRAIGHT (1st.)

FRENCH KNOT

LAZY DAISY (3st.)

OUTLINE

OUTLINE

OUTLINE (1st.)

OUTLINE

FRENCH KNOT (1st.)

FRENCH KNOT

OUTLINE

STRAIGHT

OUTLINE (1st.)

LAZY DAISY (3st.)

BULLION ROSE (3st.)

OUTLINE

FERN VARIATION (3st.)

RANDOM CROSS (1st.)

CLOSED HERRINGBONE

TWISTED CHAIN

CLOSED HERRINGBONE

LONG & SHORT

OUTLINE

SATIN

OUTLINE

OUTLINE FILLING

OUTLINE FILLING

OUTLINE

OUTLINE (3st.)

BASKET FILLING

OUTLINE

NEEDLEWORK on page 32.

2 strands, unless otherwise specified.

OUTLINE

FRENCH KNOT

SATIN

STRAIGHT

OUTLINE (3st.)

OUTLINE FILLING

OUTLINE (3st.)

OUTLINE

LAZY DAISY (3st.)

STRAIGHT (3st.)

OUTLINE (3st.)

OUTLINE

FRENCH KNOT (3st.)

SATIN

RANDOM CROSS (1st.)

BASKET FILLING (3st.)

LAZY DAISY (3st.)

FRENCH KNOT

SATIN

OUTLINE (3st.)

STRAIGHT (3st.)

OUTLINE (3st.)

OUTLINE

OUTLINE (3st.)

OUTLINE

SATIN

BASKET FILLING VARIATION

OUTLINE (3st.)

LONG & SHORT

OUTLINE

SATIN

OUTLINE (3st.)

STRAIGHT (3st.)

SATIN

STRAIGHT

OUTLINE (3st.)

OUTLINE

FRENCH KNOT

SATIN (3st.)

OUTLINE

OUTLINE

SATIN

STRAIGHT

OUTLINE (3st.)

OUTLINE FILLING

CLOSED HERRINGBONE (3st.)

OUTLINE

OUTLINE (3st.)

CLOSED HERRINGBONE (3st.)

NEEDLEWORK on page 33. *2 strands.*

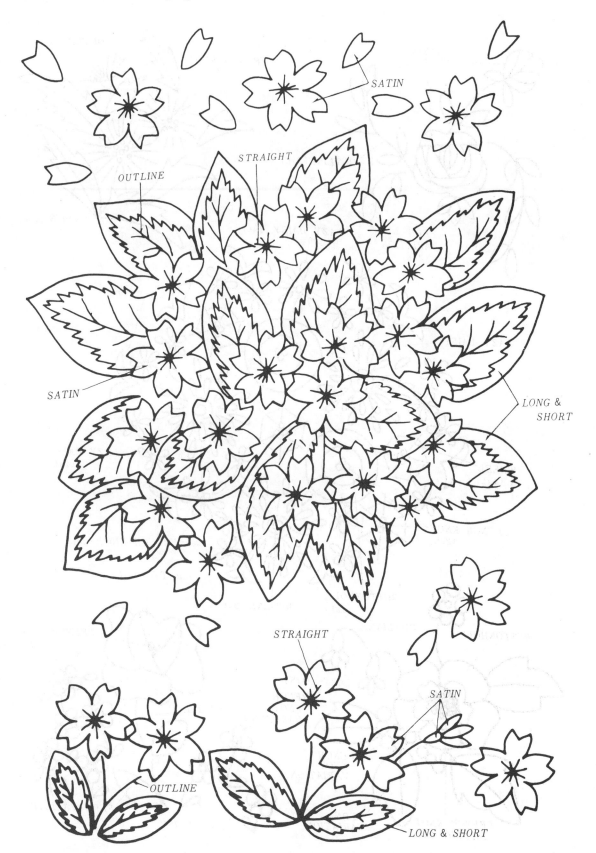

SATIN

STRAIGHT

OUTLINE

SATIN

LONG & SHORT

STRAIGHT

SATIN

OUTLINE

LONG & SHORT

3 strands, unless otherwise specified.

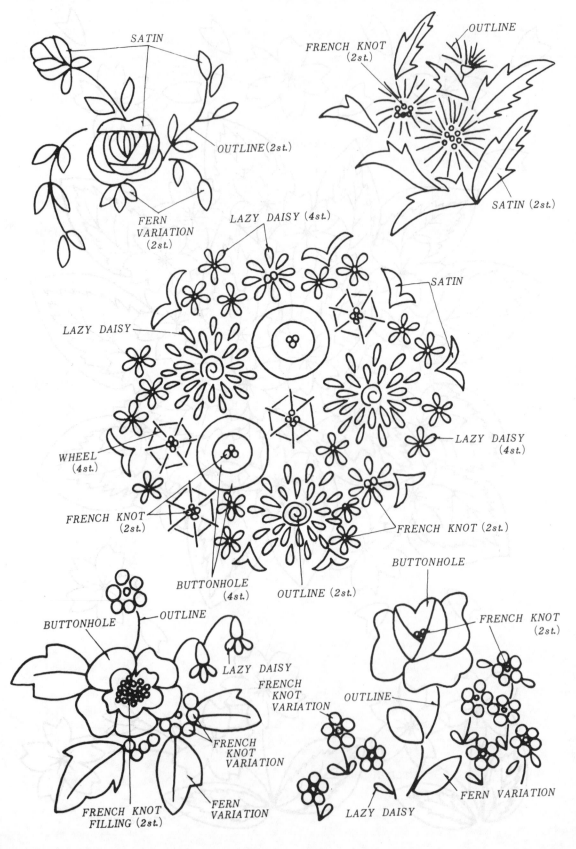

SATIN

OUTLINE

FRENCH KNOT (2st.)

OUTLINE (2st.)

FERN VARIATION (2st.)

SATIN (2st.)

LAZY DAISY (4st.)

LAZY DAISY

SATIN

LAZY DAISY (4st.)

WHEEL (4st.)

FRENCH KNOT (2st.)

FRENCH KNOT (2st.)

BUTTONHOLE (4st.)

OUTLINE (2st.)

BUTTONHOLE

BUTTONHOLE

OUTLINE

LAZY DAISY

FRENCH KNOT VARIATION

FRENCH KNOT (2st.)

OUTLINE

FRENCH KNOT VARIATION

FRENCH KNOT FILLING (2st.)

FERN VARIATION

LAZY DAISY

FERN VARIATION

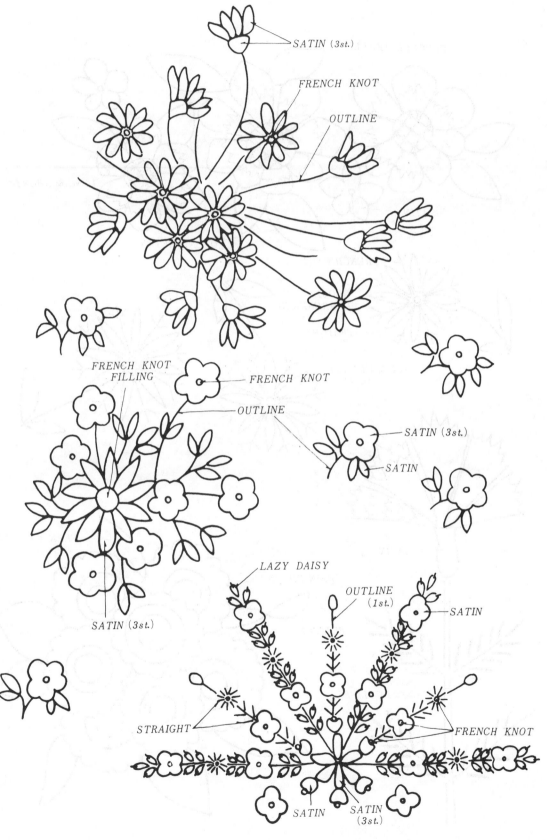

SATIN (3st.)

FRENCH KNOT

OUTLINE

FRENCH KNOT
FILLING

FRENCH KNOT

OUTLINE

SATIN (3st.)

SATIN

SATIN (3st.)

LAZY DAISY

OUTLINE
(1st.)

SATIN

STRAIGHT

FRENCH KNOT

SATIN

SATIN
(3st.)

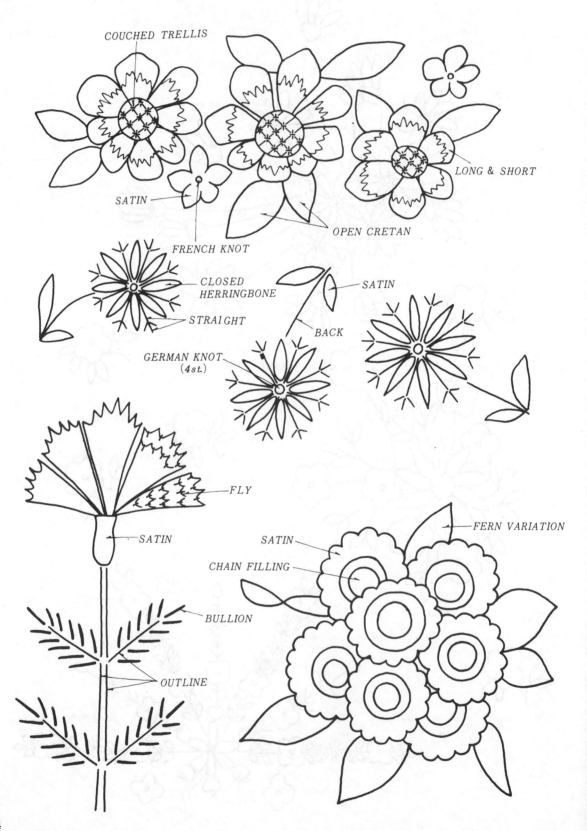

COUCHED TRELLIS

LONG & SHORT

SATIN

FRENCH KNOT

OPEN CRETAN

CLOSED HERRINGBONE

SATIN

STRAIGHT

BACK

GERMAN KNOT (4st.)

FLY

SATIN

FERN VARIATION

SATIN

CHAIN FILLING

BULLION

OUTLINE

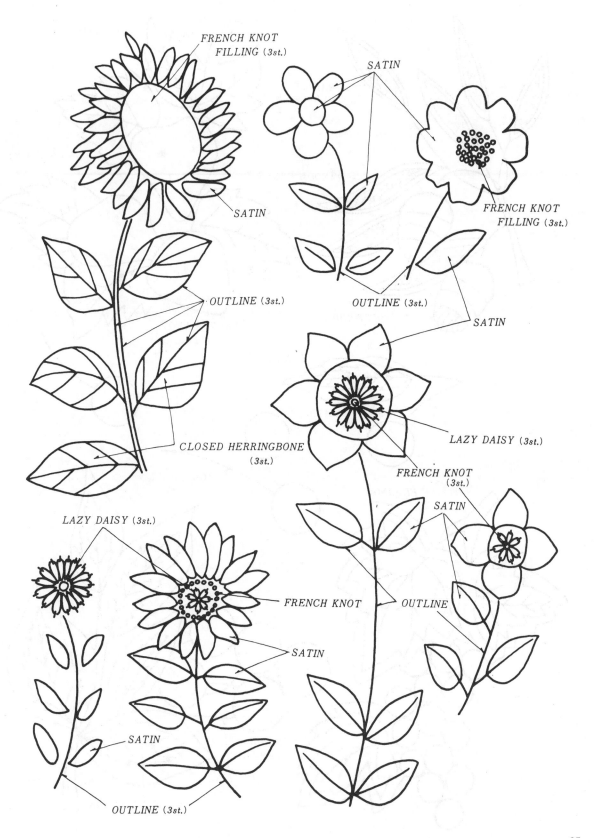

FRENCH KNOT
FILLING (3st.)

SATIN

SATIN

FRENCH KNOT
FILLING (3st.)

SATIN

OUTLINE (3st.)

OUTLINE (3st.)

SATIN

LAZY DAISY (3st.)

CLOSED HERRINGBONE
(3st.)

FRENCH KNOT
(3st.)

SATIN

LAZY DAISY (3st.)

FRENCH KNOT

OUTLINE

SATIN

SATIN

OUTLINE (3st.)

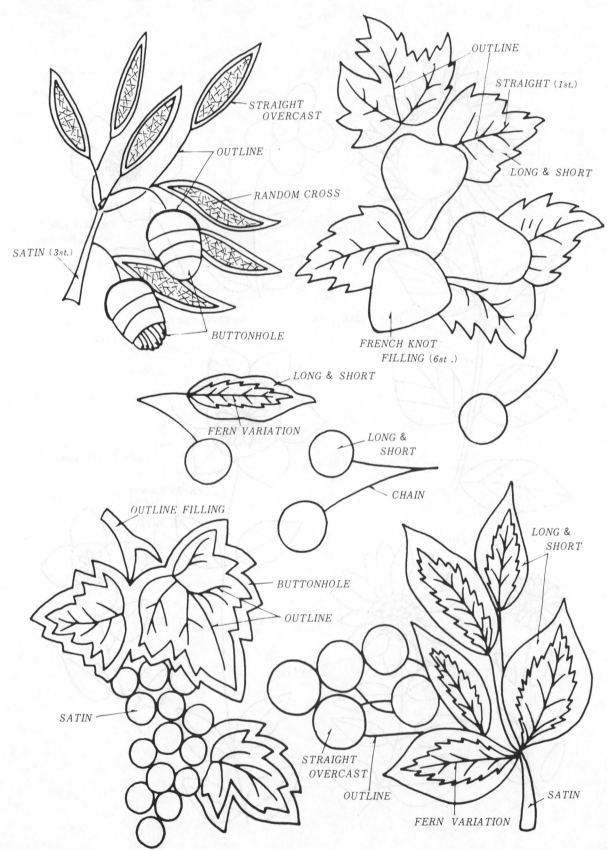

STRAIGHT
OVERCAST

OUTLINE

RANDOM CROSS

SATIN (3st.)

BUTTONHOLE

OUTLINE

STRAIGHT (1st.)

LONG & SHORT

FRENCH KNOT
FILLING (6st.)

LONG & SHORT

FERN VARIATION

LONG &
SHORT

CHAIN

OUTLINE FILLING

BUTTONHOLE

OUTLINE

LONG &
SHORT

SATIN

STRAIGHT
OVERCAST

OUTLINE

SATIN

FERN VARIATION

86

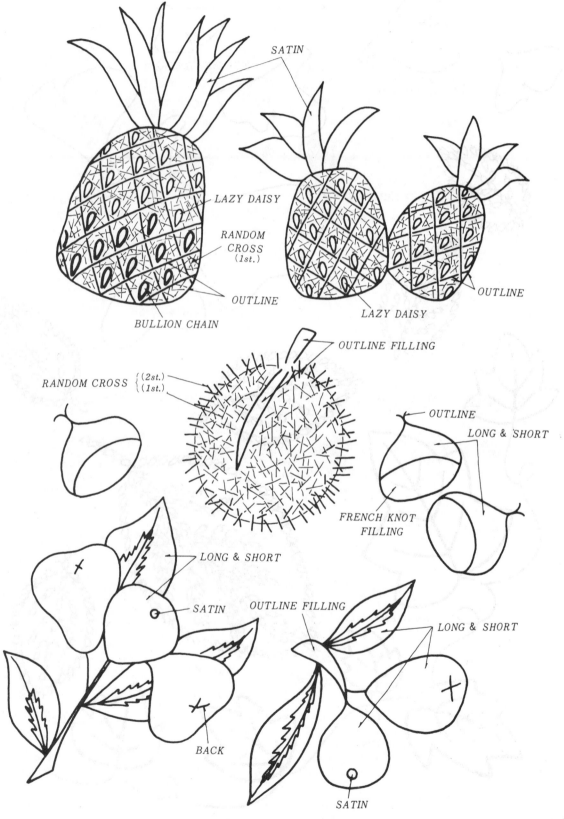

SATIN

LAZY DAISY

RANDOM CROSS (1st.)

OUTLINE

BULLION CHAIN

LAZY DAISY

OUTLINE

OUTLINE FILLING

RANDOM CROSS { (2st.) (1st.)

OUTLINE

LONG & SHORT

FRENCH KNOT FILLING

LONG & SHORT

SATIN

OUTLINE FILLING

LONG & SHORT

BACK

SATIN

CHAIN FILLING

OUTLINE FILLING

CHAIN FILLING

OUTLINE FILLING

LONG & SHORT

OUTLINE FILLING
(4st.)

LAZY DAISY

CHAIN

CHAIN

MACRAMÉ

RANDOM CROSS
(2st.)

CHAIN

MACRAMÉ (4st.)

LAZY DAISY

TWISTED CHAIN

CHAIN

MACRAMÉ

MACRAMÉ (2st.)

RANDOM CROSS
(2st.)

MACRAMÉ

RANDOM CROSS
(2st.)

RANDOM
CROSS
(2st.)

FRENCH KNOT

SATIN

LONG & SHORT
(2~4st.)

LAZY DAISY (4st.)

OUTLINE
FRENCH KNOT

SATIN (3st.)

LONG & SHORT
(2~4st.)

LONG &
SHORT
(2~4st.)

OUTLINE
(3st.)

FRENCH
KNOT

A

LONG & SHORT
(3~5st.)

LONG &
SHORT
(3~5st.)

LONG &
SHORT (2~4st.)

LONG & SHORT
(2~4st.)

SATIN (3st.)

SATIN (5st.)

LONG & SHORT
(2~4st.)

SATIN

LONG & SHORT
(2~4st.)

SATIN (4st.)

LONG & SHORT
(2~3st.)

LONG & SHORT

SATIN
(3st.)

A = *FRENCH KNOT VARIATION (3st.)*

NEEDLEWORK on page 42.

Long and short stitch, unless otherwise specified.

FRENCH KNOT
(4st.)

(3~5st.)

SATIN
(3st.)

(2~5st.)

(2~4st.)

(4st.)

FRENCH
KNOT
FILLING
(3st.)

(2~5st.)

OUTLINE
(3st.)

(3st.)

(2~4st.)

SATIN
(3st.)

STRAIGHT
(1st.)

SATIN (2st.)

STRAIGHT (2st.)

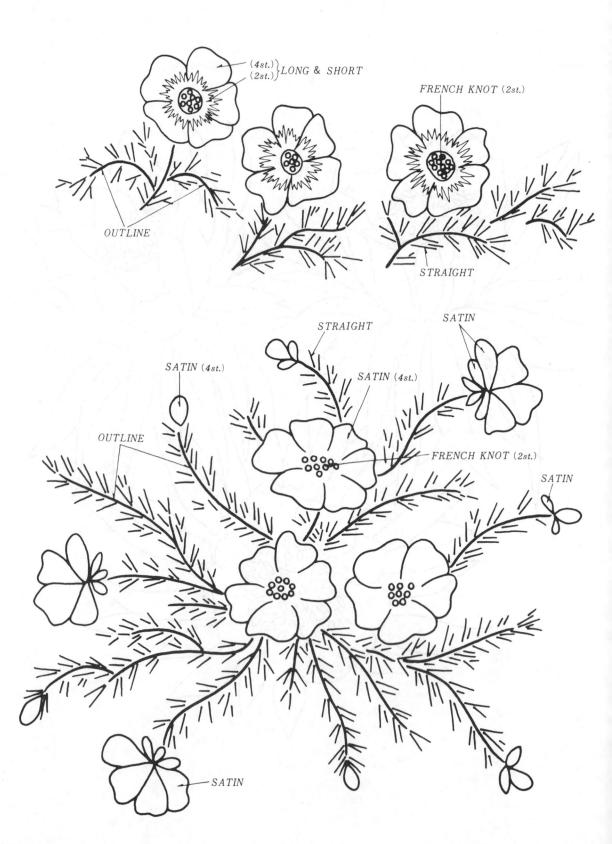

(4st.)
(2st.) } LONG & SHORT

OUTLINE

FRENCH KNOT (2st.)

STRAIGHT

STRAIGHT

SATIN

SATIN (4st.)

SATIN (4st.)

OUTLINE

FRENCH KNOT (2st.)

SATIN

SATIN

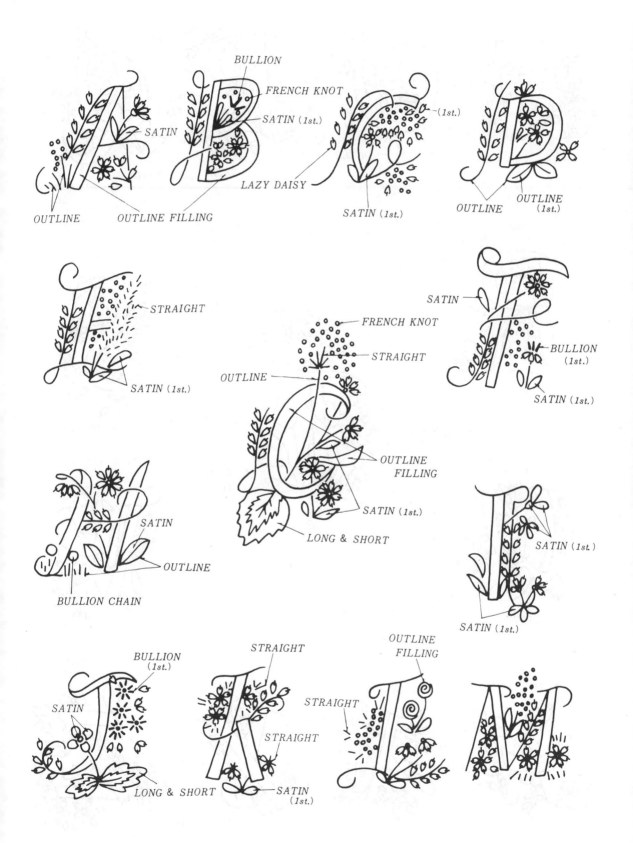

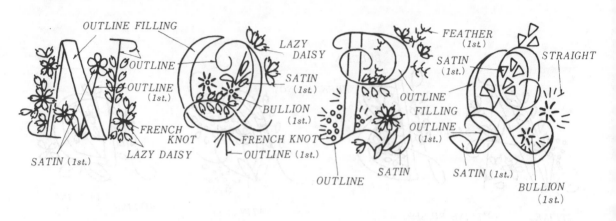

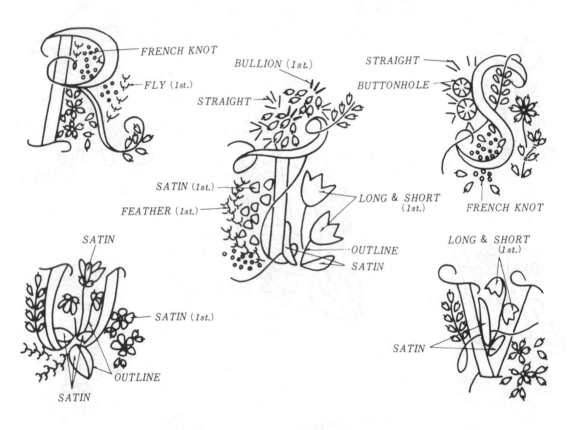

NEEDLEWORK **on page 47.** *2 strands, unless otherwise specified.*

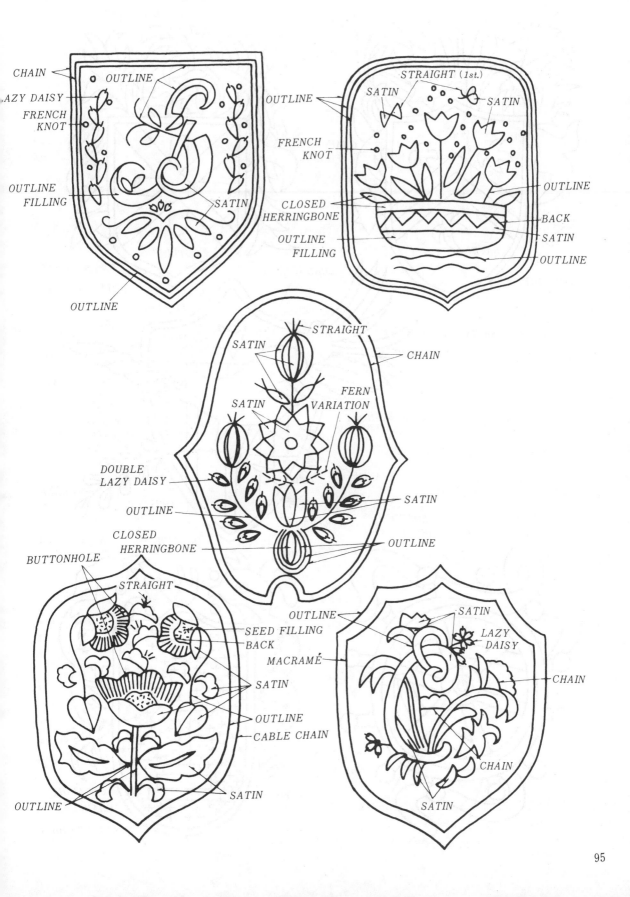

CHAIN
OUTLINE
AZY DAISY
FRENCH KNOT
OUTLINE FILLING
SATIN
OUTLINE

OUTLINE
STRAIGHT (1st.)
SATIN
SATIN
FRENCH KNOT
OUTLINE
CLOSED HERRINGBONE
BACK
OUTLINE FILLING
SATIN
OUTLINE

STRAIGHT
SATIN
CHAIN
FERN VARIATION
SATIN
DOUBLE LAZY DAISY
SATIN
OUTLINE
OUTLINE
CLOSED HERRINGBONE

BUTTONHOLE
STRAIGHT
SEED FILLING
BACK
SATIN
OUTLINE
CABLE CHAIN
OUTLINE
SATIN

OUTLINE
SATIN
LAZY DAISY
MACRAMÉ
CHAIN
CHAIN
SATIN

2 strands, unless otherwise specified.

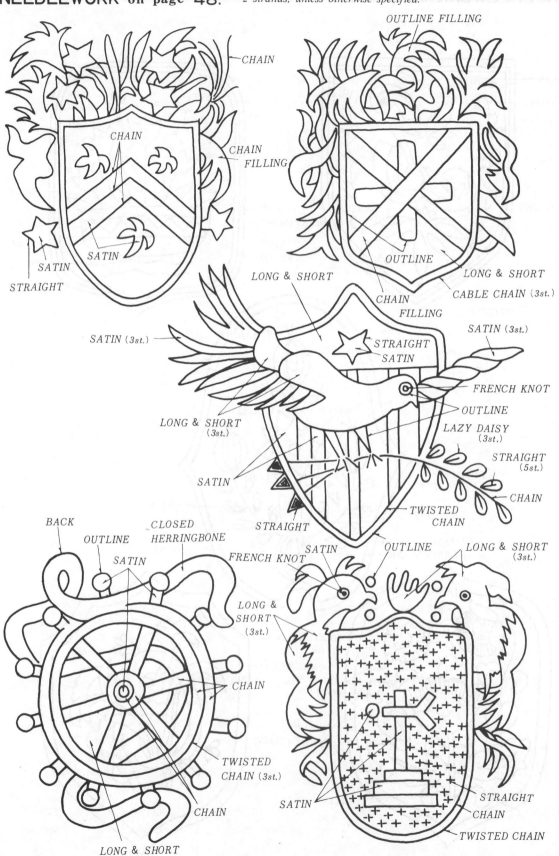

CHAIN

OUTLINE FILLING

CHAIN

CHAIN
FILLING

SATIN

SATIN

STRAIGHT

OUTLINE

LONG & SHORT

CABLE CHAIN (3st.)

LONG & SHORT

CHAIN
FILLING

SATIN (3st.)

LONG & SHORT

STRAIGHT
SATIN

SATIN (3st.)

FRENCH KNOT

OUTLINE

LAZY DAISY
(3st.)

STRAIGHT
(5st.)

CHAIN

SATIN

STRAIGHT

TWISTED
CHAIN

BACK

OUTLINE

CLOSED
HERRINGBONE

SATIN

FRENCH KNOT

SATIN

OUTLINE

LONG & SHORT
(3st.)

LONG &
SHORT
(3st.)

CHAIN

TWISTED
CHAIN (3st.)

CHAIN

LONG & SHORT

SATIN

STRAIGHT

CHAIN

TWISTED CHAIN

EMBROIDERY THREADS

THE MOST POPULAR FOR EMBROIDERY ARE No. 25 and No. 5.

No. 25—One thread consists of 6 strands, and measures 8 m per skein. You can pull out as many threads as required from the bundle if necessary (according to the design).

No. 5—Single thick thread, and is quite lustrous. One skein measures 25 m. Suitable for rough stitches.

Besides these, you have a wide variety of others such as cottons, rayons, silk, wools, even, metal threads. The sizes also range from thick, medium, fine, to extremely fine.

❁ HANDLING THE THREAD

The threads Nos. 25, 5 and 4 come in bundle or ring, depending on the manufacturer. When they are formed in a ring untie the twist, cut one end of the ring with scissors, and pull out one by one. When they are gathered together and held by one or two paper labels, pull out the length from the core of the bundle.

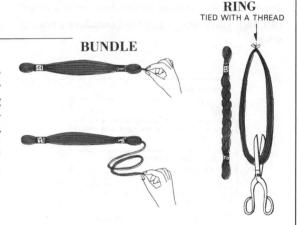

BUNDLE

RING
TIED WITH A THREAD

❁ PASSING THE THREAD THROUGH THE NEEDLE

When you pass 4 strands of the thread through an embroidery needle, fold the ends of the threads, and insert the folded edge through hole of the needle. (See illustration at right). Do the same way when you use a thick yarn like wool.

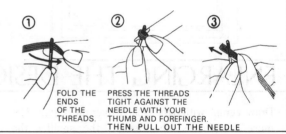

① FOLD THE ENDS OF THE THREADS.

② PRESS THE THREADS TIGHT AGAINST THE NEEDLE WITH YOUR THUMB AND FOREFINGER. THEN, PULL OUT THE NEEDLE

③

HINTS ON STITCHING

❁ HOW TO START AND END STITCHING

A securing knot is rarely made in embroidery. To start stitching, see the illustration below. If you need to make a knot, form a small loop round the needle, and gently pull out the needle, with your left thumb pressing the loop.

GENERAL STITCHING

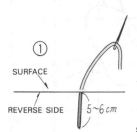

① SURFACE

REVERSE SIDE 5~6 cm

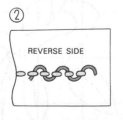

② REVERSE SIDE

SEW THROUGH THE STITCHES ON THE REVERSE SIDE (NOT SHOWING ON THE SURFACE WHEN STARTING OR ENDING THE SEAM).

FILLING STITCHING

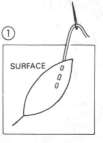

① SURFACE

SEW A FEW STITCHES TOWARD THE STARTING POINT.

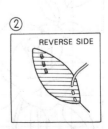

② REVERSE SIDE

SEW BACK A FEW STITCHES BEFORE BREAKING OFF (WITH CARE TO NOT SHOW THE SEAM ON FRONT).

HOW TO TRANSFER A DESIGN

Place a sheet of thin paper over the design, and copy it drawing with a hard (lead) pencil.

✿ USING TRACING PAPER

Place the waxed side of the tracing paper—the kind made for dressmaking—down on the right side of the material pinned to a board. Put the thin paper with design over the tracing paper, and work a round carefully with a steel pen, a hard pencil, or a tracing wheel.

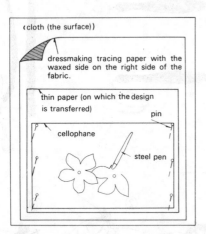

‹cloth (the surface)›

dressmaking tracing paper with the waxed side on the right side of the fabric.

thin paper (on which the design is transferred)

pin

cellophane

steel pen

✿ USING A GLASS PLATE

Bridge two boxes with a piece of opaque glass (to minimize eyestrain) and put a lighted bulb under the glass. Transfer a design found in book onto thin paper. Then put the paper on the glass, lay the material on it and outline directly on the material with a hard pencil.

✿ USING TISSUE PAPER

Trace the design onto a sheet of smooth tissue paper, and tack this into position at the edge of the background material. Using a basting thread, tack around the whole of the design through the tissue paper and material. Embroider over it, then remove the paper.

ENLARGING THE DESIGN

Draw a graph with right squares over the design. The more complicated the design, the smaller the squares. Then draw in another piece of paper the squares that are enlarged at regular rate, and trace the design in the enlarged graph. Do the opposite when reducing the design.

BASIC STITCHES

OUTLINE STITCH	**COUCHING STITCH**
CHAIN STITCH	**CABLE CHAIN STITCH**
DARNING STITCH	**MACRAMÉ STITCH**
BACK STITCH	**STRAIGHT STITCH**
TWISTED CHAIN STITCH	**STRAIGHT OVERCASTING STITCH**
SATIN STITCH	**WHIPPED RUNNING STITCH**

BASIC STITCHES

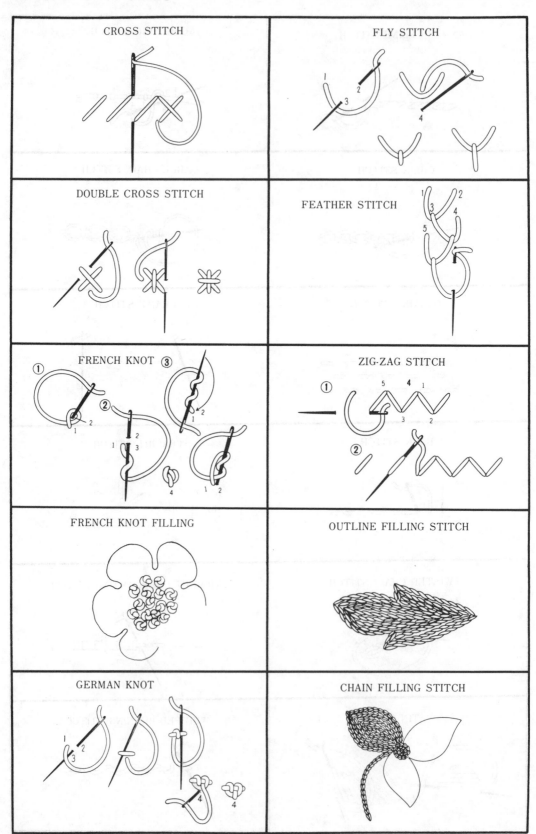

CROSS STITCH

FLY STITCH

DOUBLE CROSS STITCH

FEATHER STITCH

FRENCH KNOT

ZIG-ZAG STITCH

FRENCH KNOT FILLING

OUTLINE FILLING STITCH

GERMAN KNOT

CHAIN FILLING STITCH

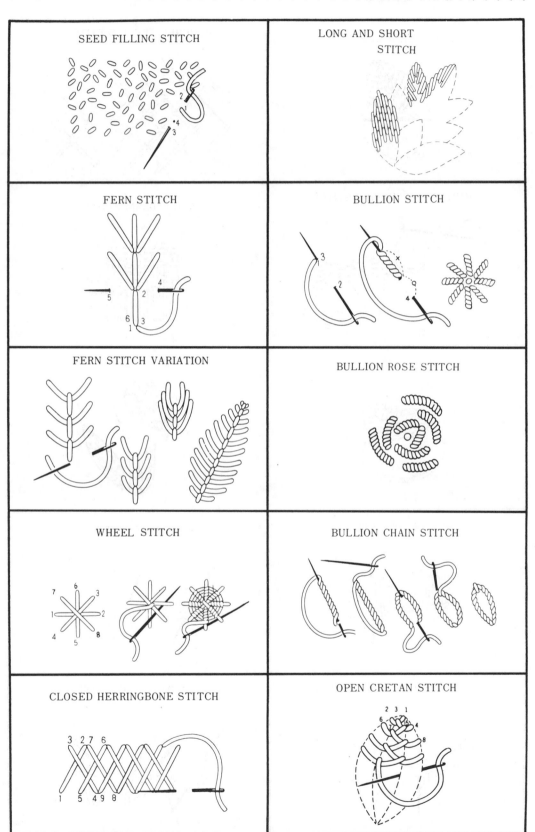

SEED FILLING STITCH

LONG AND SHORT STITCH

FERN STITCH

BULLION STITCH

FERN STITCH VARIATION

BULLION ROSE STITCH

WHEEL STITCH

BULLION CHAIN STITCH

CLOSED HERRINGBONE STITCH

OPEN CRETAN STITCH

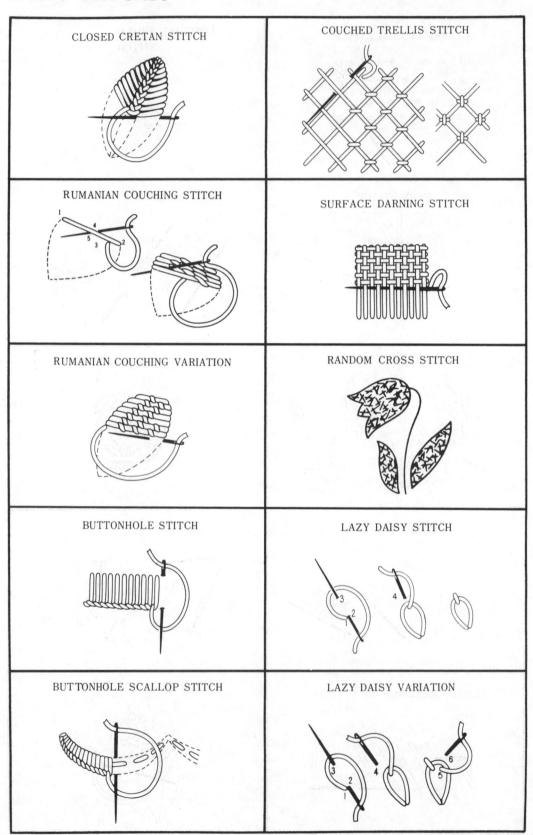

CLOSED CRETAN STITCH

COUCHED TRELLIS STITCH

RUMANIAN COUCHING STITCH

SURFACE DARNING STITCH

RUMANIAN COUCHING VARIATION

RANDOM CROSS STITCH

BUTTONHOLE STITCH

LAZY DAISY STITCH

BUTTONHOLE SCALLOP STITCH

LAZY DAISY VARIATION

DOUBLE LAZY DAISY STITCH

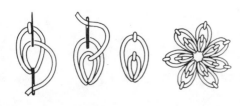

DOUBLE LAZY DAISY VARIATION

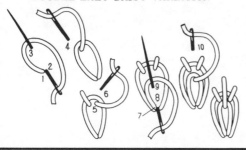

BASKET FILLING STITCH VARIATION

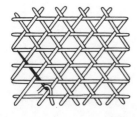

FRENCH KNOT VARIATION

FISHBONE STITCH